DISCARD

Talking About

Food and the Environment

By Alan Horsfield
and Elaine Horsfield

Gareth Stevens
Publishing

Please visit our Web site **www.garethstevens.com**. For a free color catalog of all our high-quality books, call toll free 1-800-542-2595 or fax 1-877-542-2596.

Library of Congress Cataloging-in-Publication Data

Horsfield, Alan.

Talking about food and the environment / Alan Horsfield and Elaine Horsfield.

   p. cm. -- (Healthy living)

Includes index.

ISBN 978-1-4339-3658-6 (library binding)

1. Food--Environmental aspects. 2. Food--Moral and ethical aspects. 3. Food--Social aspects. I. Horsfield, Elaine. II. Title.

TX357.H64 2010

178--dc22

2009043457

Published in 2010 by

Gareth Stevens Publishing

111 East 14th Street, Suite 349

New York, NY 10003

© 2010 Blake Publishing

For Gareth Stevens Publishing:

Art Direction: Haley Harasymiw

Editorial Direction: Kerri O'Donnell

Cover photo: iStockphoto

Photos and illustrations:

pp. 4, 5 (bottom images), 6, 7, 8, 9, 10, 11, 14, 15, 16, 17, 18, 20, 21, 22, 23, 24, 25, 27, 28, 29 iStockphoto; pp. 5 (myPyramid.gov), 19 (bottom right) courtesy Wikimedia Commons; pp. 10, 13 UC Publishing; p. 12 © Hulton Archive/Getty Images; p. 13 Coo-ee Picture Library; p. 26 Shutterstock.com; p. 30 (top right) Anthony Woodward.

Printed in the United States of America

CPSIA compliance information: Batch #CW10GS: For further information contact Gareth Stevens, New York, New York, at 1-800-542-2595.

Contents

Understanding food

What is food?

Food is anything taken into the body for the purpose of providing nourishment. Food allows living things to continue living. It usually comes from plants or animals. Food includes both solids and liquids.

Twelve thousand years ago, humans relied on hunting and gathering to find food. Food was taken directly from the natural **environment**. Today, humans modify the environment to improve the convenience of foods and reliability of their supply.

Understanding the foods you buy and the foods you eat is important. It can help you make the right food choices. It might even help you protect the environment.

When selected carefully, food provides the essential nutrients your body needs. Some foods are better than others for humans. It is important to know which food is best for you.

Different types of food eaters

Organisms, including humans, can be divided into three groups: **carnivores**, **herbivores**, and **omnivores**.

Carnivores are meat eaters and can be **predators** or **scavengers**.

Many animals are predators and hunt for food in the natural environment.

Humans, as predators, have learned to raise animals for slaughter, often on a large scale.

Did you know?

This pretty little sundew is a carnivore. It traps small insects on its sticky leaves and then slowly digests them!

Omnivores eat parts of plants, but generally only the fruits and vegetables produced by fruit-bearing plants. They also eat animals. Most people, as omnivores, eat a variety of foods to remain healthy. They require a balance of plant and animal foods.

Carnivores are animals that get their food from killing and eating other animals. Carnivores mainly eat herbivores, but they can also eat omnivores and other carnivores. Carnivores need a lot of energy to hunt and kill other animals. The bigger the carnivore, the more animals it has to kill for its food.

Carnivores and omnivores are important to the **ecosystem**. They keep other species from becoming overpopulated. An ecosystem needs many more herbivores and omnivores than carnivores to remain in balance.

mypyramid.gov

The U.S. government has set guidelines for a healthy diet. Eat a variety of foods using the suggested proportions.

What foods should people eat?

To maintain body weight, food eaten must be balanced with physical activity.

Herbivores are animals that get their energy from eating only plants. You will usually see these animals, such as cattle and sheep, grazing all day. This is because they need to eat a lot to meet their energy demands. If you have a lot of herbivores in your ecosystem, you will need very large areas of plants, especially grasslands.

I'll eat almost anything!

5

Linking food to the environment

A **food chain** shows the food relationship between living things in the environment. It shows how energy and nutrients are transferred from plants (producers) to herbivores to carnivores and then to decomposers. All play a role in keeping a balance in nature. With large-scale food production and an ever-increasing world population, that balance is under threat.

The sun provides energy for almost all living things on our planet.

Producers include all green plants. They make their own food. Producers harness the sun's energy to make food. Living things depend on plants for oxygen and food. Plants produce the bulk of the food in food chains and webs.

Consumers are organisms that eat other organisms. They include: herbivores, carnivores, omnivores, and parasites (animals that live off other organisms and harm them).

Decomposers include bacteria, molds, and **fungi** that convert dead matter into gases to be returned to the air, soil, or water. Decomposers are very important. They break down dead organic matter and **recycle** nutrients to be used again by producers.

Without decomposers, Earth would be littered with dead plants and animals.

Herbivores are primary consumers. There need to be more herbivores than carnivores to keep an environment in balance.

Carnivores are secondary consumers. They eat the herbivores.

A food chain describes a single, simple pathway of food energy, like links in a chain. There is one type of organism per link. A food chain usually starts with a primary producer (plant) and ends with a decomposer. An example of a simple marine food chain:

Start here

algae
(tiny sea plants) → small crustaceans
(crabs, lobsters) → fish → squid

↓

death and decay
(bacteria) ← sharks ← seals

Vertical food chain

grass
↓
grasshopper
↓
frog
↓
snake
↓
eagle
↓
bacteria
(digest dead matter)

Food webs

Most food chains are interconnected. Animals usually have a varied diet and, in turn, become food for a variety of creatures that prey on them. These interconnections create food webs. The arrows in this simplified web show how food energy moves.

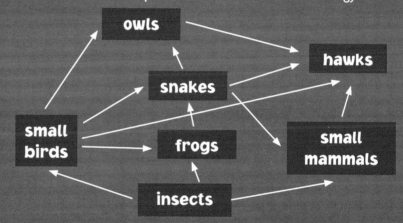

Plant and animal communities are everywhere. They are on farms and in ponds, forests, and backyards. Members of these communities depend on each other to survive.

Producers and consumers depend on one another. Some provide food, some clean up the waste, and some spread seeds. Others provide shelter, and some provide oxygen or carbon dioxide for the community.

Human communities are expanding so fast that they often force animals and their natural communities into extinction.

Humans demand more food

Over time, as the human population grew, it demanded more food than the local environment could provide. So people began to modify their environment. The key way they did this was to replace the local vegetation with food crops that produced more food. The effects of planting food crops were eventually felt around the globe. Four basic food crops—wheat, corn, rice, and potatoes—became the most popular foods throughout the world.

Wheat

Wheat is a grass that is grown worldwide. It is one of the most important human food grains.

There is evidence that wheat was grown 10,000 years ago.

About 5,000 years ago, wheat was planted in North Africa, Spain, and Ireland. One thousand years later, wheat reached China.

Did you know?

In the eighteenth century, planting seeds in rows replaced spreading seeds by scattering the grain.

Corn

Corn (or maize) is a grain that was probably first cultivated in Central America, about 10,000 years ago. Cultivation then spread throughout North and South America around 1500 B.C. Corn cultivation was spread to the rest of the world in the late fifteenth century.

Corn can grow to a height of many yards (m), with four ears on each stalk.

Worldwide, more corn is grown than any other crop. The United States produces almost half of the world's harvest.

Did you know?

Corn would not exist if it weren't for people. It does not exist naturally in the wild and can only survive when cultivated.

Every year, thousands of acres of land are bulldozed in regions that can grow wheat. Land clearing and wheat farming can lead to erosion and soil problems. They also contribute to the loss of plant and animal species.

Rice

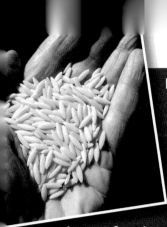

Rice is a grass, native to tropical and subtropical Asia and Africa. It has long slender leaves, and it grows to about 6 feet (1.8 m) tall.

Rice is the staple diet for a large part of the world's population, especially in Asia. It is the most consumed cereal. It is the world's third largest crop.

Growing rice is suited to countries with low labor costs and lots of water for the young plants. In Asia, rice is often grown in paddy fields and on terraced hills. Water in the paddies stops weeds from choking the crops. The water is drained when the rice is ready to be harvested.

Did you know?

Rice paddies are an important habitat for birds, amphibians, and snakes.

These animals prey on insect pests that damage the rice.

Potatoes

The potato is a tuber (it forms under the ground) and is the fourth most important food crop in the world.

Potatoes originated in the Andes Mountains of Peru and Bolivia. They have been grown for at least 2,400 years. Strangely, the potato took a long time to reach North America.

The Spaniards took it back to Spain in the sixteeth century. It then made its way to Italy and northern Europe, then to Bermuda and the early colonies of North America.

The potato is about 80 percent water and 20 percent solid. Potatoes have a greater yield per acre than grain crops.

Did you know?

The potato is a relative of tobacco, peppers, eggplants, and tomatoes.

Fruit and vegetables

Depending on whom you ask, the term "fruit" has many meanings. Fruits are how flowering plants, especially trees, spread seeds. For consumers, fruit usually refers to plants whose fruits are sweet and fleshy (oranges and apples).

Nuts, grains, and many vegetables are the fruit of the plant they come from.

Vegetables are often **annuals**. They are more savory than fruit and often cooked as a main course.

Nuts (edible seeds) may grow under the ground (peanut) or on trees (walnuts).

Fruits, vegetables, berries, and nuts were all collected by early gatherers, before there were gardens and orchards.

An early record of bananas goes back to Alexander the Great's conquest of India (327 B.C.) when he first saw bananas.

Did you know?

Bananas don't grow on trees! The banana plant is a giant herb.

Fungi

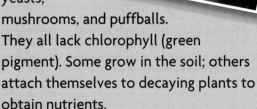

Fungi are a group of organisms that includes molds, mildews, yeasts, mushrooms, and puffballs. They all lack chlorophyll (green pigment). Some grow in the soil; others attach themselves to decaying plants to obtain nutrients.

Because they lack chlorophyll, they can be any color except green. They cannot use the sun's energy.

Some varieties of fungi are poisonous. People have been eating some fungi for thousands of years.

Did you know?

Fungi are special. They are not plants or animals. They may grow in soil like plants, but they take their energy from the environment like animals, not directly from the sun.

Dairy and meat-producing farms need a huge amount of land. Grazing animals eat all day long, and grass will only grow as fast as the environment allows. As the human population grows, more land is cleared for dairy and meat production. This affects native animals and plants.

Dairy products

Dairy products are those foods produced from milk.

It is unknown when humans began milking their animals. Milk products, especially cheese and yogurt, changed people's lives. They provided food when the growing season was over and hunting and gathering were difficult.

Did you know?

Louis Pasteur (1822–1895), a French microbiologist and chemist, is famous for finding how to stop milk and wine from going sour. This process is called pasteurization.

Meats

Meat is the tissue of animals, including birds, reptiles, snails, and sea creatures.

Humans have always hunted. Cave paintings around the world show the hunting of animals for food, clothing, and shelter.

Red meat (such as beef or lamb) is the muscle of animals, often reddish before cooking.

White meats include poultry and fish.

Did you know?

Farmers need to feed their cattle 8 pounds (4 kg) of grain to produce 1 pound (.5 kg) of meat. They need to feed their pigs about 4 pounds (2 kg) of grain to produce 1 pound (.5 kg) of pork.

A major threat to the environment is animal waste, which can pollute waterways. Dairy cattle produce methane and nitrous oxide, which are released from their manure. Both are greenhouse gases. Free-range cattle often destroy the banks of streams and rivers. Factory farms depend upon large "lagoons" to contain animal waste. Spills from lagoons can create health risks and pollution problems in waterways. Debate continues about animal welfare issues and "smell" pollution.

DEMAND FOR FOOD AFFECTS OUR ENVIRONMENT

Native Americans

Early Native Americans were hunters and gatherers. They ate food that was nutritious and available locally. They knew which plants could be eaten, which were tasty, and those good to use as a medicine. They knew the best times to harvest. This knowledge was passed down through the generations.

Their hunting methods kept them moving from one hunting area to another. Thus, they never completely depleted all the animals from one area.

Animal numbers quickly increased once the Native Americans moved to a new area to hunt. Sometimes, hunting involved burning areas to drive out the animals. This affected small areas at a time. But over centuries, this created entirely new types of landscapes.

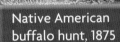

Native American buffalo hunt, 1875

Early settlers

The early European settlers didn't understand the local environment. Because they didn't know what plants could be eaten, they often came close to starving. Many explorers actually died from thirst and starvation when there were edible plants and water nearby. Settlers didn't have the local knowledge to find or catch food. They removed the local vegetation and replaced it with crops and animals brought from their native countries. That meant clearing forests and grasslands to plant crops or provide pasture for livestock.

Jamestown colony, around 1615

Settlement and growth

Since European settlement, the focus has been on the needs of food production, urban development, transportation, and industry.

Some farming methods damage the land, environment, and waterways. Large tracts of land are now barren and useless. Even those in use rely on fertilizer to build up soil nutrition.

The growth of farming has reduced many fish habitats. This is especially true in rivers and in the breeding areas of river estuaries. As the water from the rivers runs to the sea, it takes with it soil, nutrients, and fertilizers. Fertilizers that end up in the sea provide "food" for algae. As masses of dead algae decompose, they use up the oxygen in the water, harming ocean life.

The fishing industry must search further out into the ocean to get fish to feed the growing population. Some species are now extinct because they have been overfished.

clearing land and planting crops, early 1900s

Cooking food needs energy

Cooking food, whether in the home or a factory, uses energy. Wood fires were initially used to cook food. As populations grew, more wood was needed for cooking. Trees were used faster than they could be replaced. Wood fires are poor sources of energy. They also cause air pollution and can be a health hazard. In many places, they are banned.

Coal replaced wood as a major energy source but still caused air pollution.

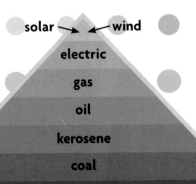

The energy pyramid

(cleanest fuel at the top to the dirtiest fuel at the bottom)

solar → ← wind
electric
gas
oil
kerosene
coal
wood

Geography and air pollution

Many cities around the world have air-quality problems. Geography combined with air pollution causes serious health issues. For example, cities located in valleys have less air circulation than cities in wide-open spaces. Mountains trap the pollutants, which can mix with the air people breathe and the rain that falls. Though governments and health agencies work together to promote "cleaner" energy sources, conditions are still poor enough in many places that air-quality warnings are issued on particular days.

Larger cities required more energy, and electricity was a great clean, efficient solution—at least for the towns and cities using it. However, the electricity needed to be generated. First, coal generated electricity, then oil was used. Now nuclear energy produces much of the energy used around the world.

How to save energy when cooking

- Microwave ovens cook food three times faster than standard ovens. They save up to 70 percent of electricity used for cooking.

- Fan-forced ovens cost 35 percent less to run than conventional ovens. They force the heat evenly throughout the oven, reducing your cooking time by one-third.

- Pressure cookers and electric grills use about half the energy of an oven.

- Use pots and pans with flat bases that closely fit the size of the burner.

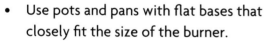

Population growth requires new ways of working

Through history, people have changed the environment to produce more food. At first, a family farm could produce enough for the family and a few neighbors, perhaps even a small town. But as population increased, family farms could not meet the demand. Larger, more efficient farms raised more crops and animals. More food and better transportation made feeding people in towns and cities possible. In most industrialized countries, farming and food production cover more land area than any other industry. Huge factories process the food into whatever people demand. Large rail and road transportation networks bring the food to the local supermarkets.

Where does food come from?

The fridge.

The development of large farms has resulted in the loss of forests. It has also meant there is a greater risk of erosion. Poor soil quality is often the result of increased use of fertilizers, herbicides, and insecticides. Dams and flood control have meant the death of many waterways and wetlands. The habitats of many species are now under threat.

Concerns about truck transportation include noise pollution, dangerous exhaust emissions, and the safety of all road users.

transportation

market

supermarket

In the United States, transportation accounts for 28 percent of greenhouse gas emissions each year. The transportation emissions have increased 29 percent since 1990.

More people need more water to drink

Although water is not a food, it is essential to life. It is important in cooking and essential in food production and processing.

Water, water everywhere, but not much left to drink

Basic human requirements include food, shelter, and water.

Some countries have begun projects to remove salt from ocean water to combat water shortages.

Bottled water—where does it come from?

Spring water comes from underground. Most spring water is carried in tankers to the bottling plant. More often than not, it is not bottled at the lovely place in the ads! Some of it is even chemically treated.

Artesian water comes from deep underground. Some of it has been there for thousands of years. It can be undrinkable.

Did you know?

The water we use is very old. It has been around forever! It is continually being recycled and reused.

Much precious drinking water is lost because of dripping taps.

Dam water

Dams have been responsible for:

- flooding farm valleys
- changes to animal and plant habitats, both in the dam and downstream from the dam
- turning rivers into sluggish streams

Many people with rainwater tanks say their water tastes better than a community's public water. Could this be so?

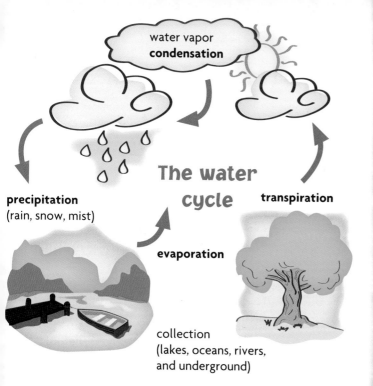

water vapor
condensation

The water cycle

precipitation
(rain, snow, mist)

transpiration

evaporation

collection
(lakes, oceans, rivers,
and underground)

Earth has a limited amount of water, and that water keeps going around and around in a "water cycle."

The quantity of water on Earth does not change—just the quality! The quality of the water we drink is being made unsafe by pollution.

Water from the sea?

To produce desalinated water, large amounts of energy are needed as well as expensive equipment. It is very costly compared to the use of freshwater from rivers.

Too much salty waste returned to the ocean can harm sea life.

Most fruit and vegetables, as well as produce such as rice and sugar, come from irrigated areas. Some of these are in low rainfall areas.

Field irrigation

We should drink plenty of water every day!

Food please, but hold the chemicals

There is high demand for foods that don't use any chemicals when they are produced. Organic foods do not use chemicals such as pesticides or artificial fertilizers. They contain no artificial ingredients. The growing process is trying to copy what it was like growing food in the natural environment before people added chemicals and fertilizers to grow more food and grow it more quickly.

Organic farmers grow fruit and vegetables, legumes, and grains. They also produce meat, dairy foods, eggs (which are free-range rather than from caged hens), and honey.

Organic farming

Animals raised using organic methods are treated humanely. For example, chickens are free-range and not kept in cages, and cows are not kept in feed lots. Animals are also not fed any growth-regulating drugs.

Organic
COFFEE
AND
FOOD

ORGANIC CARROTS

Does it really taste better?

Organic food is allowed to ripen naturally so the full flavor is attained. Some people tasting organically grown food for the first time notice that it tastes different and has more flavor. Others don't notice a difference.

Why eat organic?

There is more evidence to suggest that chemicals in our food have an effect on the health of children. Many diseases have been linked to additives and chemicals in food. Cancer patients may be advised by doctors to eat organic food. Children are often sensitive to additives in food.

It is what *hasn't* been added to organic food that makes it good for you. It is the most natural way of growing food and rearing animals.

How do I know it is organic?

Organic farms are only certified after they have been following organic principles for three years. The use of the word "organic" is regulated by the government. It is important to look for the certification logos when buying organic food. The main one in the United States is "USDA Organic." In Canada, the logo is "Canada Organic."

Organic farming helps the environment

Organic farming helps protect the land. No chemicals or pesticides end up in the soil. Crop rotation and natural fertilizers are used. This helps keep the soil, as well as anything grown in it, healthy.

Genetically modified foods

As the world population grows, it needs more food. The more food, the more the environment is used for food production. More chemicals and fertilizers are needed. The more crops you grow, the more insects you need to kill with pesticides. One solution to these problems is to make the food resistant to insects. Today, we are able to genetically modify crops and animals. They can be changed so they produce more and are more resistant to insects and disease.

What are genetically modified (GM) foods?

"GM" is the term used when technology alters the genetic makeup of living organisms such as animals, plants, or bacteria. Combining genes from different organisms may result in a new organism, which is said to be genetically modified.

Why create GM foods?

GM foods are created for many reasons.

Crops

- o makes the food taste better
- o creates better quality
- o increases the amount of food from the same area
- o improves resistance to disease

Animals

- o increases resistance to disease
- o grows more food from the same animals
- o improves the health of the animals

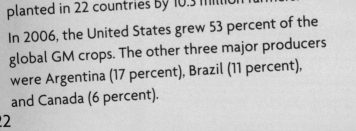

Are GM foods common?

In 2006, a total of 252 million acres of GM crops were planted in 22 countries by 10.3 million farmers.

In 2006, the United States grew 53 percent of the global GM crops. The other three major producers were Argentina (17 percent), Brazil (11 percent), and Canada (6 percent).

Some of the GM crops available today are insect resistant, such as soybeans, corn, cotton, canola, and alfalfa. There is also a rice being tested with increased iron and **vitamins**.

In the near future, fish might mature more quickly and cows might be resistant to mad cow disease.

The GM industry claims that GM foods will ensure there is enough for our growing populations.

Why all the protests against GM foods?

Growing GM foods poses some risks. Environmentalists believe that the impact of GM food on the natural environment is not known. How can you keep the seeds of a GM crop from blowing to other crops or into the native vegetation? They also claim the planting of GM crops will destroy a wide range of plants and animals.

Are GM foods safe?

GM foods are new to humankind. Governments therefore are very cautious when assessing if they are safe for humans to eat.

The total effects of GM foods on human health are unknown. The effects may include allergic reactions and building up resistance to antibiotics in humans. Campaigners against GM foods want proof that GM foods will not harm people before they support GM foods.

Sugar, water, and dental issues

Teeth are tools used for eating. With our teeth, we can bite, slice, and grind our food.

To do this, we have four different types of teeth.

Tooth type	Location	Number	Use
incisors	at the front	8	cutting
canines	to the side	4	tearing
bicuspids	near the back	8	grinding
molars	at the back	12	grinding
	Total =	32	

Sugarcane and sugar beet are the main sources of "table" sugar. Sugar is one of the most widely traded commodities in the world. The United States is a major exporter of sugar, with large areas of sugar grown under irrigation. All "sugars" (including those that occur naturally in fruits and in honey) promote tooth decay to some degree.

Don't expect fluoride to win the fight against decay all by itself. You have to play your part by keeping your teeth and gums healthy.

Fizzy drinks

It is not always the high levels of sugar in many sports drinks or fizzy (carbonated) drinks that are the main reason for decay. It is the acidity of certain products that causes the problem.

Drinking "diet" versions of fizzy drinks reduces sugar consumption, but these products are still very acidic.

How to care for your teeth

If your teeth do not need special attention, it is quite simple to care for them.

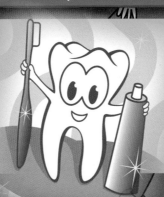

Many dentists recommend the use of **fluoride** toothpaste.

Eating a variety of natural and unprocessed foods will help keep your teeth strong.

24

Sugarcane and the environment

The growing of sugarcane in many countries has caused the removal of rain forests and other environments.

Growing sugarcane has been responsible for reducing wildlife species and polluting rivers and seas. It has also caused soil erosion, air pollution from burning cane, and damage to coral reefs.

Some people believe that too much sugar is being produced. We are eating more than we need.

Being sensible

It makes sense to limit sugary foods that don't have much nutritional value; for example cakes, cookies, lollipops, and sugary drinks. Instead, eat plenty of fruit, vegetables, and cereals.

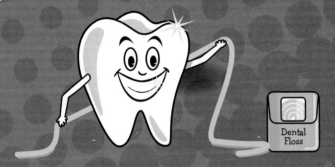

Dental Floss

Although sugar heads the list for causing decay, it is not the only cause. How you eat and how well you care for your teeth are also important. Frequent snacking on starchy foods or foods you sip or suck for some time can result in a trip to the dentist.

Bottled water

Most bottled water does not contain fluoride. Many people prefer bottled water, claiming it is wrong to add anything to water supplies. Others believe that fluoridation causes problems such as allergies, bone fractures, and cancer.

Many people feel that drinking bottled water is a threat to the environment because of the distance it is transported as well as the use of plastic bottles.

Not all bottled water comes from "pure" spring water. The "fine print" may contain the initials PWS—public water source!

Tap water from public supplies is safe to drink—and cheaper. Bottled water is more expensive than gasoline!

What is fluoride?

Fluoride is not a medication. It occurs naturally in the environment—in rock, soil, plants, and water sources. Water fluoridation is the addition of fluoride to a water supply to prevent dental decay. Seawater can contain much higher levels of fluoride than is found in community water supplies.

Foods all wrapped up

Prepackaged and **convenience foods** are foods that have been partially or fully prepared for eating by a manufacturer. Look at the displays at the local grocery store or push a cart down the supermarket aisle. You will see shelves of packaged convenience foods that need little preparation and cooking. Anyone pressed for time can have a tasty meal in moments. Just watch the ads! There are plenty of choices, from precut salads to microwave meals and meals in cans or vacuum packs. The consumer (that's you) is so far removed from the food source that you no longer even know how some food is made and what is in it.

It's a fact

People are becoming more dependent on convenience and take-out foods. An increasingly large part of household budgets is spent on these foods. Pizza and soft drinks are the favorites.

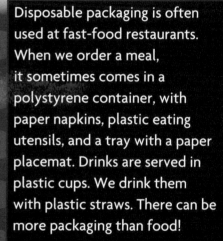

Disposable packaging is often used at fast-food restaurants. When we order a meal, it sometimes comes in a polystyrene container, with paper napkins, plastic eating utensils, and a tray with a paper placemat. Drinks are served in plastic cups. We drink them with plastic straws. There can be more packaging than food!

Many of us only use the napkin for a few seconds. If you calculate the amount of time a disposable product is used, you may think it is hardly worth the resources used to produce it!

Convenience foods and packaging

Convenience foods may come in metal, glass, plastic, or paper containers. Americans produce millions of tons of household packaging each year, much of it for food products. Packaging usually ends up in landfills. Plastic accounts for 25 percent of total landfill and takes a long time to break down.

City growth means waste

Large amounts of waste are created by people eating food. More waste is created through building, operating, and maintaining towns or cities. Millions of tons of solid wastes are received and disposed of at landfills each year. One estimate suggests that an average person creates about 1,400 pounds (600 kg) of waste each year.

The major problem with creating waste is how to dispose of it and the impact this will have on the environment. Landfills are the most common form of waste disposal around the world. However, they take up land that could be used for other purposes.

Some cities and towns oppose having new landfill sites nearby. Although the U.S. Environmental Protection Agency has laws meant to keep landfill sites safe, who wants one in their backyard?

ZERO-WASTE COMMUNITIES

People are choking their natural environment on the millions of tons of waste that they produce each year. Some communities around the United States and the rest of the world have aimed to become "zero-waste" communities. This means one person's waste is a valuable resource for someone else. Reduction, reuse, and recycling are important parts of these programs. Even the smallest community's actions can have a big impact on the world.

Waste Disposal	
Method	Problem
Landfills	limited space, smell, scavengers spreading disease
Incineration	chemicals released into the air, contaminated ash
Storage	leaking of chemicals

Reduce, reuse, recycle

The Three R's for caring
for the environment

REDUCE
REUSE
RECYCLE

People produce a lot of waste products. Much time and effort go into recycling that waste. Even with all this effort, mountains of waste remain.

Waste is also produced by nature. However, what is made as waste by one plant or animal is usually used by another. Nature recycles the waste so it is not wasted!

How is that so?

Try this simple experiment.

Breathe in. You have breathed in air, which is a mixture of gases. Air contains about 20 percent oxygen and a tiny amount of carbon dioxide.

Breathe out. You have breathed out air that contains less oxygen but more carbon dioxide.

You have just taken part in one of nature's cycles! The oxygen you breathed in was the waste product of plants. The plants use your waste—carbon dioxide—to make their food.

Dead plants and animals can also be called waste. Leaves rot on the ground because of fungi and bacteria. Dead animals are consumed by animals and bacteria. Droppings become food for plants and some animals.

Because waste in nature is recycled, it does not build up. Nature continually renews itself unless there is interference in the cycles of life, death, decay, and renewal.

As long as the sun shines (supplying energy), nature can go on recycling its resources. In this way, Earth's limited resources can be used over and over again!

The carbon cycle

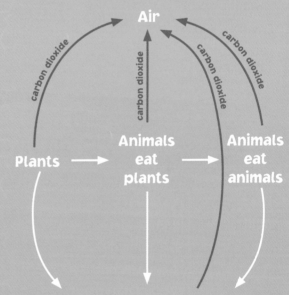

The burning of crops destroys this process.

Much of our food comes in a variety of plastic containers.

Most types of plastic can be recycled.
The number in the recycle triangle refers to the type of plastic. In some places, different numbers must be recycled separately. Use your recycle bins correctly and do the right thing.

What is the difference between nature's waste and humans' waste?

Nature's waste is biological waste. Humans produce other types of waste. Not much is reused.

Household food scraps can be recycled.

Composting is natural and inexpensive, and it is great for the garden.

You have selected a compost bin that sits flat on the ground. What do you do next?

1. Select a site. The best site is one that has good drainage and is shaded in summer.

2. Select your compost materials. Compost is a mixture of different things:

- nitrogen-rich kitchen organics (fruit and vegetable peelings, fresh green garden organics, weeds, green leaves, and manure)

- nitrogen-poor brown garden organics (dry leaves, paper, straw)

Don't add meat or dairy products.

3. Layer the materials. Start with a thick layer of coarse mulch at the base for drainage.

Then follow the three simple steps.

Step 1. Add a thin layer of kitchen and green garden organics.

Step 2. Cover this layer with "brown" waste.

Step 3. Moisten well. (Not too wet!)

Add a sprinkling of soil.

Then repeat the three steps.

4. Maintaining your compost. Add air to the compost by turning the material over with a garden spade. Alternatively, you could have a worm farm. Worms love most kitchen scraps. (Don't use meats or dairy products.)

Did you know?

Americans produce millions of tons of waste each year. The waste includes household garbage and industrial waste, which is created by things we buy or use. It's becoming more difficult and expensive to find new places to dispose of our waste.

Percentage of household wastes in the United States

28%	plastic, metals, other materials
7%	glass
18%	yard waste
40%	paper
7%	food scraps

Food words

Our environment is not just our physical world. It includes all living things as well as the society we live in and the culture that surrounds us. Our total environment shapes the way we survive.

People depend upon food to survive. It has always been a part of our culture. Popular stories, poems, songs, and plays about food have existed in every place and age. As early humans usually lived in close contact with animals, it was natural to invent stories describing the adventures of animals. In ancient Greece, Aesop was one such person.

The fable of the sour grapes

A fox, wandering through the forest, became hungry and thirsty. On reaching a small cottage in a clearing, he spied a trellis with a grapevine growing over it. High in the vine hung a large bunch of ripe, round, juicy grapes.

The fox couldn't reach the grapes, so he tried jumping up and grabbing them. Every time he tried, he missed. He became more and more frustrated. He finally gave up, muttering that the grapes were probably sour anyway.

Moral: People should not blame circumstances when their lack of success is a result of their own failure.

Aesop

Those grapes are sour!

Jack Sprat

Jack Sprat could eat no fat,
His wife could eat no lean,
And so betwixt the two of them
They licked the platter clean.

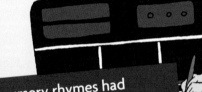

Many nursery rhymes had hidden meanings.
Check out: www.rhymes.org.uk/jack_sprat.htm to discover what this rhyme might really be about.

Coffee and tea

Molly, my sister, and I fell out
And what do you think it was all about?
She loved coffee and I loved tea
And that was the reason we couldn't agree.

Coffee and tea have not always been **traditional** drinks in Europe.

They only became popular after traders returned with them from distant lands. People changed from thinking about local foods to considering foods from distant environments—foods that had to be transported huge distances.

Glossary

annuals	plants that grow once (usually once per year) and then die; they do not reshoot and grow the following year
carnivores	animals that eat other animals
condensation	the change from vapor to liquid
convenience foods	foods prepared partially or fully by manufacturers
ecosystem	all the living organisms (plants, animals, and microbes) linked together in an environment
environment	all the physical, biological, social, and cultural conditions that surround an organism and affect its form and the nature of its survival
evaporation	liquids, including water, turning to vapor without being boiled
fluoride	a chemical that is used to protect teeth from decay
food chain	a series of different living things, each of which feeds on the one below
fungi	living organisms, neither plant nor animal, which contain no chlorophyll
herbivores	animals that feed on plants
omnivores	animals that eat both plants and other animals
organisms	living things
precipitation	moisture from the air that falls to the ground
predators	animals that hunt and kill other animals for food
recycle	use of unwanted materials and waste for other purposes
scavengers	animals that feed on dead and rotting flesh and discarded food scraps
traditional	based upon ideas that have been passed down through generations
transpiration	moisture passing from living organisms into the air
vitamins	organic substances used in small quantities, vital for life

For Further Information

Books

Allen, Julia, and Margaret Iggulden. *Food and the World*. New York: Franklin Watts, 2008.

Franchino, Vicky. *Genetically Modified Food*. Ann Arbor, MI: Cherry Lake Publishing, 2008.

Web Sites

Kids Organic Club
www.organics.org/kids_club.php

Planet Protectors Club for Kids
www.epa.gov/osw/education/kids/planetprotectors/

Publisher's note to educators and parents: Our editors have carefully reviewed these Web sites to ensure that they are suitable for students. Many Web sites change frequently, however, and we cannot guarantee that a site's future contents will continue to meet our high standards of quality and educational value. Be advised that students should be closely supervised whenever they access the Internet.

Index